D0297515
LM 1336221 6 S

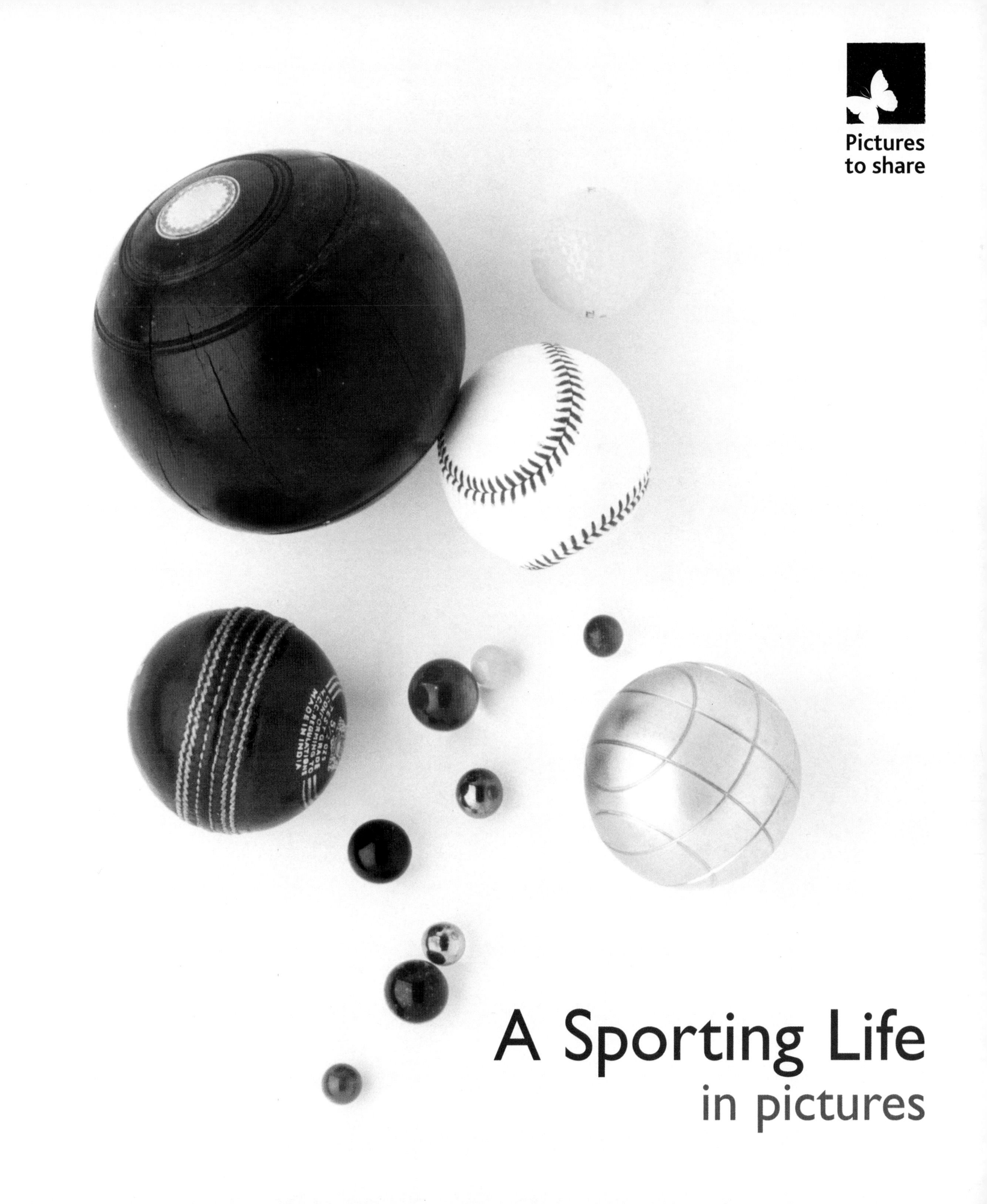
Pictures to share
A Sporting Life
in pictures

For Peter and John,
two true sports fans.

L B LAMBETH LIBRARIES	
LM13362216	
BERTRAMS	16/11/2012
R796	£17.50
S	

Pictures to share

First published in 2008 by
Pictures to Share Community Interest Company,
a UK based social enterprise that publishes
illustrated books for older people.

www.picturestoshare.co.uk

ISBN 978-0-9553940-6-5

Front Cover: Line-out. All hands reach for the ball during the Hospital Rugby Cup final between London Hospital Rugby XV and Bart's Hospital XV.
© Derek Berwin/Hulton Archive/Getty Images

Endpapers: Snooker game © Ann Bridges

Frontispiece: Sports balls. © Dave King/Dorling Kindersley/Getty Images

Title page: Boy Scout Philip Halloran in the group's car 'Blazaway III' in which he won the Soap Box Derby at Weston-Super-Mare, England. © Hulton Archive/getty Images

Back cover: Detail from Royal Ascot © thoroughbredphoto.com
Driver G. Abecassis © H F Davies/Hulton Archive/Getty Images
Football boots in ceramics © Janet Halligan

A Sporting Life

in pictures

Edited by Helen J Bate

training

It isn't the mountains ahead that wear you out,

it's the grain of sand in your shoe.

Photograph: Woman running with Border Collie.
© Tony West/CORBIS

Quotation: Unknown

cricket

Cricket to us
was more than play,

It was worship
in the summer sun.

Photograph: Watching a cricket match on the village green at Oxted, Surrey.
©Evening Standard/Hulton Archive/Getty Images

Quotation from 'Pride of the Village' by Edmund Charles Blunden (1896-1974)
Quoted in 'The Penguin Cricketers Companion' (1978)

Twins playing cricket in
Ivor Novello's garden

© Sasha/Hulton Archive/Getty Images

highland games

When you win,

nothing hurts

Photograph: A man throwing the Scottish hammer at the Glenfinnan Highland Games, Scotland.
© Jim Richardson/National Geographic/Getty Images

Quotation: Joe Willie Namath b. 1943

greyhound racing

Don't let's go to the dogs tonight

For mother
will be there.

Main photograph: Dog Handlers with their Greyhounds at the reopening of the Belle Vue racetrack in Manchester in 1927 © Hulton-Deutsch Collection/CORBIS.
Small photograph: Mr C Hopkins with his trophy-winning coursing dogs. © A R Coster/Hulton Archive/Getty Images.

Quotation from 'Don't Let's go to the Dogs Tonight.' 1926 by Sir Alan Patrick Herbert (1890-1971)

SPORTING CHRONICLE
GREYHOUND RACING

Photograph: Two men fishing on a jetty, Belgium.
© Benelux/zefa/CORBIS

I believe
every human has
a finite number
of heart-beats.

I don't intend
to waste any
of mine running
around doing
exercises.

Painting: 'The Fisherman', detail of a man fishing, 1884 Oil on canvas by Jean Louis Forain. (1852-1931)
©The Bridgeman Art Library/Getty Images

Quotation: Neil Armstrong, US astronaut and first man on the moon.

Please don't ask me what the score is.

I'm not even sure what the game is.

Photographs: A boy watching a cricket match at the Oval, London, from the top of a lamp post. © H F Davies/Hulton Archive/Getty Images

Quotation: Ashleigh Brilliant (contemporary writer) www.ashleighbrilliant.com

horse racing

In June 2008 Richard Hills rode Aqlaam in the Jersey Stakes at

Royal Ascot

Aqlaam is trained by William Haggas from Newmarket

Photographs: ©thoroughbredphoto.com

R. Hills
5
Ascot

Dance

like a butterfly

Sting

like a bee.

Photograph: Portrait of boxer Muhammad Ali at a press conference at the Waldorf Astoria Hotel, Manhattan, New York, December 15th 1977.
© CBS Photo Archive/Hulton Archive/Getty Images

Quotation: 'Catchprase' of Muhammad Ali (previously Cassius Clay)

rock climbing

Overcoming the challenges

makes life worth living.

Photograph: Rock climbing at Owens River Gorge.
© Kelly Harriger/CORBIS

Quotation: Mary Tyler Moore (1936 -)

football

In 1966

Captain Bobby Moore led England's football team to a 4-2 victory over West Germany at Wembley Stadium.

Small photograph: Football boots in ceramics © Janet Halligan
Main Photograph: © Stringer/Hulton Archhive/Getty Images

What a polite game tennis is.

Painting: 'Portrait of Max Decugis' (oil on canvas) by Francois Flameng (1856-1923)
The Bridgeman Art Library/Getty Images

Quotation: J M Barrie (1860-1937)

The only time I'm for

the high jump

is when I'm in trouble
with the wife!

Photograph: A high jump demonstration at a summer school for organisers of physical education.
© Fox Photos/Hulton Archive/Getty Images

Quotation: Anonymous

It is not only

fine feathers

that make fine birds.

Painting: 'Pigeon' by Clive Uptton (1911-2006)
Private collection/© Look and Learn/The Bridgeman Art Library
Quotation: Aesop (620 BC-560 BC), from The 'Jay and the Peacock'

motor racing

The ideal man bears
the accidents of life
with dignity and grace,
making the best of circumstances.

Photograph: Driver G. Abecassis narrowly misses a lake
at the Crystal Palace road circuit in London. © H F Davies/Hulton Archive/Getty Images

Quotation: Aristotle (384 BC-322 BC)

12

diving

Female underwater **diver** looking at corals, sponges and fish in the Fiji Islands.

© A. Witte/C. Mahaney/
Stone/Getty Images

Mud! Mud! Glorious mud!

Nothing quite like it for cooling the blood.

Photograph: Wales and Italy, Women's International Rugby, Glamorgan Wanderers RFC, Cardiff. © Andrew Orchard / Photolibrary Wales

Quotation from 'The Hippopotamus' (1952)
by Michael Flanders (1922-75) and Donald Swan (1923-94)

ice skating

Our greatest glory
is not in never falling,
but in getting up every time we do.

Main photograph: A skater at Hollow Ponds, London has cushioned himself against a fall in the severe winter of 1927-8 © Fox Photos/Hulton Archive/Getty Images.
Small photograph: Ice dancer, Margo McMenemy showing off her skating skills. © Maurice Ambler/Hulton Archive/Getty Images

Quotation: Confucius (551 BC-479 BC)

Painting: Victorian card with English Fox Hunting scene 1919 by Frantz Charlet
© Swim Ink 2, LLC/CORBIS

CHARLET
19

cycling

Life grants nothing to us mortals without

hard work

Photograph: Cycling competitor on the 1:5 gradient in the 40th Annual Hill Climbing Championships of England at Brasted Hill in Kent.
© Underwood & Underwood/CORBIS

Quotation: Horace (65 BC-8 BC), 'Satires'

Life's truest happiness

is found in friendships
we make along the way.

Photograph: Golfers on a course © Rob Howard/CORBIS

Quotation: Anonymous

Acknowledgements
Our thanks to contributors who have allowed their
text or imagery to be used for a reduced or no fee.
Thanks also to all those who assisted in the development
of this book by helping with or taking part in trials.

All effort has been made to contact copyright holders.
If you own the copyright for work that is represented, but have
not been contacted, please get in touch via our website.

Thanks to our sponsors

Some quotations have been provided by
'Chambers Dictionary of Quotations',
Chambers Harrap Publishers Ltd, 2005
and www.quotationspage.com

All rights reserved. No part of this publication may be
transmitted in any form or by any means, electronic or
mechanical, including photocopying, recording or any
storage and retrieval system, without the prior
permission in writing from the publisher.

Published by
Pictures to Share Community Interest Company.
Peckforton, Cheshire
www.picturestoshare.co.uk

Printed in England by
Burlington Press, Station Road, Foxton
Cambridgeshire CB22 6SA